The Simple Step By Step System Anyone Can Use to Create Generational Wealth

WES YOUNG

The Simple Step By Step System Anyone Can Use to Create Generational Wealth

The Simple Step By Step System Anyone Can Use to Create Generational Wealth

Wes Young

Free 7-day generational wealth course at
GenerationalWealthBooks.com

Title: The Simple Step By Step System Anyone Can Use to Create
Generational Wealth

Author: Wes Young

Publisher: Pageville Press

Cover Design: Madison Young

ISBN: 9780980190731

Copyright © 2023

Free 7-day generational wealth course at
GenerationalWealthBooks.com

Table of Contents

Page:

9 - Guilt

13 - Why I Want You to Create Generational Wealth

19 - The Big Promise

23 - How to Make Creating Generational Wealth
Inevitable

27 - The Step By Step Generational Wealth System

31 - The Power of 70-10-10-10 Plus 1

35 - How I Developed the Generational Wealth System

39 - A Deep Dive into 70%

43 - Use Money to Make Money

53 - Save and Invest in the Future

59 - Make the World a Better Place

63 - Plus 1

69 - Work Your Generational Wealth System Every Day

73 - Generational Wealth Challenges and How to
Overcome Them

77 - When to Start?

Free 7-day generational wealth course at
GenerationalWealthBooks.com

79 - How to Start Immediately

81 - Action and Consistency Are the Keys that Unlock
Generational Wealth

83 - The Power of Accountability

87 - How to Get Help Creating Generational Wealth

89 - Teaching Your Kids How to Create and Maintain
Generational Wealth

93 - What Generational Wealth Is Not

97 - How to Get the 7 Day Generational Wealth Course
for Free

99 - Will You Please Help Me Make the World a Better
Place?

101 - About the Author, Wes Young

Guilt

Why are you interested in creating generational wealth?

It's easy to say that everyone wants more money. And while that's true, that's rarely a good enough reason to put in the work required to create generational wealth.

It's not the first thing that comes to mind for most people, but guilt is a driving force in 1 way or another for most people I help create generational wealth.

And even if some people won't admit that guilt might be driving them, it still works in the same way.

My experience with creating generational wealth 100% started with guilt.

My journey has grown to include much more than guilt. But guilt is what made me finally quit messing around and get serious about creating generational wealth.

I've read that guilt isn't good. But if you use guilt the right way, it propels you to something bigger and better.

The generational wealth system in this book works whether guilt about something made you start on this journey, or if your reasons are because of something else.

But I'm here to tell you that if you're starting your journey to creating generational wealth because you feel guilty, you're not alone.

My journey really got started when I read a Bible verse. It stopped me in my tracks and made me take a hard look at my life.

Here's the Bible verse:

Proverbs 13:22

"A good man leaveth an inheritance to his children's children."

When I read this verse, I was fairly successful. But I realized I didn't really have anything to leave as an inheritance to my children and their children.

I was flooded with guilt.

At that point I had 2 choices. I could continue piling on the guilt, or I could start doing something about it.

I chose to start doing something about it immediately.

If you're not starting your journey to creating generational wealth because of guilt, I'm still happy to have you along on the ride.

But if you're starting because of guilt, do the same thing I did.

Choose to use your guilt to make changes. Use the guilt to propel you to building the generational wealth that you can be proud to leave to your children and their children and everyone you love.

Free 7-day generational wealth course at
GenerationalWealthBooks.com

If you have children, you want better things for them. My children have always been taken care of, but I'm building generational wealth that they can continue to grow.

And more importantly, I'm giving them a system for creating and growing generational wealth to teach their children and children's children.

This is the same system I'm sharing with you in this book.

Let's get started.

Why I Want You to Create Generational Wealth

Hello. My name's Wes. I'm truly excited for you to start on your journey to creating generational wealth with me.

But before you get started, I want to give you a big **WARNING!**

I know you want to jump right in and learn how the generational wealth system works. But don't give in to the temptation to jump ahead. The chapters at the beginning of the book are important building blocks to make creating generational wealth almost inevitable.

Once you finish this book from beginning to end, you can go back and read the chapters that you're working on again. You can use the book as a reference book to help you stay on track on your journey to creating generational wealth.

But start with a solid foundation so your journey has the best chance of succeeding. These first few chapters build a solid foundation.

You hold everything in your hands that you need to start your journey. This isn't one of those books that give you just enough information to get excited, but doesn't give you everything you need. I include every step of the generational wealth system in this book.

I know this system works because I've used it and helped my clients use it. If you follow the step by step system and make a commitment to never give up, you're going to succeed.

I want you to create generational wealth. In fact, I want everyone I know to create generational wealth.

An important part of the generational wealth system is using a small part of your wealth to make the world a better place. You're going to learn more about this in the chapter about making the world a better place.

I know that the more people there are creating generational wealth; the better off the world is going to be. And the more wealth you create, the more people you can help.

I'm going to introduce you to something that's not common in books like this. I'm going to tell you the truth about everything in the generational wealth system and why I wrote this book.

Some people don't really want to hear the truth. But I've found the people I work with and help that have the most success want nothing but the truth. You can only make the progress you at to make looking at things as they really are.

The truth is it doesn't matter if you like me or not. If you use the system in this book, your life is going to be better than it was before. So, even if I don't resonate with you through my writing, don't miss the opportunity to learn and use this system that can change your life and the lives of everyone you love.

Free 7-day generational wealth course at
GenerationalWealthBooks.com

Here's a list of every reason I want you to create generational wealth, and why I wrote this book and started a YouTube channel about generational wealth.

- I want you to create generational wealth to make the world a better place.
- I have a mission that includes many things. One of the things in my mission is to make the world a better place. I'm doing things in my life that does this. But the more people there are making the world a better place the better.
- Here's the truth part that usually gets left out or glossed over. I make money by helping people create generational wealth. I make a few dollars when someone buys my books. But I spend that money on selling more books. However, the thing I enjoy doing most is consulting with people who want to create generational wealth and entrepreneurs. I have multiple streams of income, but consulting is my favorite. It's labor intensive because I'm trading my time directly for money. And I have limited time. But the truth is that the more people I introduce the generational wealth system to, the more people come to me for help. So, consulting is one of the ways I create generational wealth for myself and my family.
- The more I help people create generational wealth, the more money I make. Once you see the value included in this book and put what you learn into action, the more you're going to realize how large your return on investment is. This $10

Free 7-day generational wealth course at GenerationalWealthBooks.com book can be worth millions to you. And when you want a little help with any part of the system, you're going to use me to help. I'm giving you as much value as I know how in this book. And many people will follow the system and create generational wealth. But you might need a simple 15 or 20 minute phone call to give you the push you need. Or you might be like some of my clients and want to talk once a week or every other week. Or you might want to use me for accountability.

- I want you to sign up for the free 7 day generational wealth course that's a companion to this book. It gets you started immediately and guides you through the complete system in 7 days. And after the 7 day course, I send additional information to help you on your journey. And yes, every once in a while I'm going to offer you something that you can buy if it helps you on your journey. But you never have to buy anything else to make the system work. And you can stop receiving emails from me at any time. Even if you plan to stop receiving my emails after the course, at least get the 7 day course first. Once you see how much value I'm providing in this book, the easier it's going to be to see that I want to help you. And the 7 day course is going to help you.

There you have it. You know every reason why I want you to create generational wealth and why I wrote this book.

Free 7-day generational wealth course at
GenerationalWealthBooks.com

Give me the opportunity to give you value before you make any decisions. That value starts with this book.

If you're ready to get started creating generational wealth, read the rest of the book and start your journey to creating generational wealth immediately. And then get the free 7 day course. Complete details are included later in this book.

Let's get started.

The Big Promise

I can't promise you're going to create generational wealth because I don't know what you're going to do and what you aren't going to do. I also don't know exactly what generational wealth means to you.

Some people simply want to create enough wealth that they can forget about financial stress and take care of their family. Others want to create a vast empire that they can pass down to their children and grandchildren.

Many different paths lead to generational wealth. And everyone has unique skills and talents and abilities.

Some people build and run big businesses. Others build and run small businesses. Others develop and use high income skills and invest their money wisely to create generational wealth. And others buy and sell things for a profit or sell things for other people and build wealth.

I obviously can't cover every way you can create generational wealth in a book because there are 1,000's of ways to do it.

But what I can give you is a simple step by step system that I have used and others have used to build generational wealth. And if you know how other people do it and you use the same system they use, the only missing ingredients are dedication, action, and consistency.

Here's my big promise to you.

Free 7-day generational wealth course at
GenerationalWealthBooks.com

You can use the simple system in this book to create generational wealth. I know it's true because I've seen it work time and time again.

If you follow the steps in this system and are determined to never give up and keep taking action, your odds of creating generational wealth are almost infinitely better than they are right now.

And no matter where you end up, you're going to be better than you are now.

You might be tempted to skip some of the things in the system. I strongly suggest not skipping anything in the system until you see how well the system works.

Eventually you're probably going to make some adjustments to the system. In other words, you're going to make the system your own.

And over time, your goals may change. Even when you reach a point in your life when you have created generational wealth, you might want to continue working on your life and wealth.

Here's a personal example. While I follow the 70-10-10-10 plus 1 system explained in my book, I'm still striving to improve. I want to get to 10-20-60-10 or 10-40-40-10.

In other words, I'm working towards being able to live off 10% of my income. I'm not there yet, but as long as I'm working on it, making progress every day, and following the proven system, getting there is almost inevitable.

Free 7-day generational wealth course at
GenerationalWealthBooks.com

Speaking of inevitable, the next chapter is about how to make creating generational wealth inevitable. I'm sure you're ready to get to the meat of the system, but don't skip the next chapter. It's important.

How to Make Creating Generational Wealth Inevitable

Do you want to make creating generational wealth inevitable?

You might have tried many different ways to generate wealth and/or success before and didn't achieve the results you wanted.

I've done a lot of things and chased success and money for decades. I've had varying levels of success. But everything I've done and everything I've learned has been important.

Every time I failed I learned something. And every time I succeeded I learned something.

Eventually I learned to model what I wanted to accomplish on what other people do that accomplish what I want to accomplish. This was a big breakthrough.

Once I learned how to model success and saw how powerful this process was, things started falling into place.

And this is how I developed the generational wealth creation system in this book. I know this system works because others have used it before I came along. They might not have used it exactly like I use it, but the processes are the same.

I know my generational wealth system works because I use it and my clients use it and we're getting results.
Free 7-day generational wealth course at
GenerationalWealthBooks.com

If you want to make creating generational wealth inevitable, here are the exact steps you need to put in place.

1. Decide you want to develop generational wealth.
2. Determine why you want to create generational wealth.
3. Commit to creating generational wealth. This means you never give up, no matter what. There's no other option.
4. Use the generational wealth system in this book. This system has been proven to work, so it will work for you.
5. Take action every single day. You have to work on your generational wealth every day. The plus 1 part of the system is just as important as every other step.
6. Evaluate your progress on a regular basis, and make adjustments as needed.
7. Get accountability.

I cover all of these steps in this book. And every step is important.

Creating generational wealth is not easy. But the process is fairly simple. By the time you finish this book you will have the simple process and framework you need.

I cover this in much more detail later in this book, but you have to take action every day. All of the knowledge in the world won't do you much good if you never take action.

Free 7-day generational wealth course at
GenerationalWealthBooks.com

You have to take action and work on your generational wealth plan even on the days you don't feel like it. If you don't feel good, you still need to get your plus 1 in every day. If nothing seems to be working and you want to give up, you need to take action anyway.

Your mindset has as much to do with creating generational wealth as anything else. You can decide to create generational wealth and follow through or you can decide to continue getting the same results you're getting now.

You can commit to creating generational wealth or continue getting the results you're getting now.

The reason why you're reading this book is because you're not happy with the results you're getting now.

And don't skip the second thing on the list. Determining the reason or reasons why you want to create generational wealth is a big part of achieving what you want.

While part of the reason why I'm creating generational wealth is for me, the more important reasons are for my family and because I'm making the world a better place.

It's ok if your first thought is you want to create generational wealth for you. But I recommend digging deeper and finding the thing or two that mean so much to you that they will keep you moving forward on your path to generational wealth when everything looks dark.

Free 7-day generational wealth course at
GenerationalWealthBooks.com

My family and my quest to make the world better keep me going when things go sideways.

Yes, I'm on this journey for me. But I'm also on this journey for my family and the world. The thought of failing and letting my family down is a driving force.

I use this driving force to keep taking action and building every day.

Now, find your driving force or forces and use them to keep you moving toward generational wealth every day.

The final point I want to touch on in making creating generational wealth inevitable is the last one on the list.

You need to find a way to get accountability. I cover this more in another chapter, but being accountable to someone is another tool you can use.

You need to use every tool you have to create generational wealth.

Whether you use someone like me to hold you accountable or find someone else creating generational wealth and holding each other accountable, as long as you get accountability your odds of achieving generational wealth go up considerably.

The Step By Step Generational Wealth System

In this chapter I'm going to give you the complete step by step generational wealth system. And in the following chapters I take a closer look at each part of the system.

Don't worry about what you think you can do and what you might not think you can do as you learn about this system. I've worked with a lot of people using this system and I've helped people from all walks of life learn and use it.

The most common issues are:

- I can't make ends meet on 100% of my income, so how can I possibly survive on 70% of my income?
- I don't have any idea of how to use money to make money.
- How can I create generational wealth if I give away part of my income?

I give you a complete roadmap for all of these situations, and more, in the following chapters. I also cover these topics and many other bumps in the road in the free 7 day course.

This system works whether you're starting with nothing, or worse, or whether you're starting from a position of financial strength.

Don't cheat yourself out of a system that will change your life. You can do this, no matter where you are right now. Focus on learning how the system works in this chapter and keep your mind open.

The generational wealth system includes 5 main parts. I call the 5 parts the 70-10-10-10 plus 1. Here's a quick overview of each part.

The first part is using 70% of your income (all of the money you have at your disposal, wherever it comes from) for all of your expenses and spending. This includes entertainment and discretionary spending.

The second part is using 10% of your income to make money. There are many different ways to do this, but you're using 10% of your income to increase your income. I cover several ideas to help you get started in the chapter on this part.

The third part of the system is using 10% of your income to save or invest for your future. You can save and invest in many different ways.

The fourth part of the generational wealth system is using 10% of your income to make the world a better place. You can give the money to causes that are important to you or help people in need.

The fifth part is what I call the plus 1 part of the system. Plus 1 means that you work on your generational wealth system at least 1 hour every day.

Free 7-day generational wealth course at
GenerationalWealthBooks.com

Eventually you're going to work on your generational wealth system more than 1 hour a day. But at first you dedicate at least 1 hour every day to keep you on track while the system starts working.

If you truly want to create generational wealth, you can dedicate at least 1 hour every day and make sure you invest the time no matter what's going on in your life.

That's the complete generational wealth system. Remember 70-10-10-10 plus 1 to keep how the system works in your mind.

Once you see how the system works by putting it into action, your life will start changing. It can be almost like magic how everything starts falling into place.

In the next chapter you're going to learn a little bit more about the power of this system.

The Power of 70-10-10-10 Plus 1

The generational wealth creation system I use and teach has 5 main parts. And each of the 5 parts is equally important.

When you combine all 5 parts and they start working together, the magic starts happening.

The power of this simple system is once you get things moving in the right direction, the entire system becomes habit. You're going to start automatically doing the things you need to do every day to keep growing.

You might be skeptical about how everything in the system works right now. Or you might be skeptical that you can use the system to create generational wealth.

And no matter how many times I say you can do it, you're going to have to prove it to yourself.

But once you put all 5 steps in action and start seeing results, your momentum will build.

Something that most systems don't address is your mindset. The truth is that your mindset is going to change on your way towards creating generational wealth.

I can talk about your mindset forever and it's not going to change much. But once you see how the system works and how it's working for you, your mindset will shift.

I discuss this more in the chapter about making the world a better place, but it's the perfect example so I'm covering it here as well.

From a logical standpoint, it doesn't make much sense to give away money if you're trying to create generational wealth. But the more you're able to give away and use your money to make the world a better place, the more wealth and opportunities come your way.

I recently read a quote that said something like, if you don't think having more money will make you happy, then you haven't given enough money away.

In other words, having more money lets you help more people. And when you start helping more people and making the world better, your mindset shifts.

Most people have a scarcity, or lacking, mindset. This mindset was the biggest thing I had to overcome to start creating generational wealth.

But once I learned how to create generational wealth, using the system in this book, my mind made an important shift. Instead of looking at every penny I gave away or used to improve the world as a burden, I figured out that I can generate more wealth.

And the more I use to improve the world, the more I have.

But, you can't fully believe this because I said it. You have to prove it to yourself.

Free 7-day generational wealth course at
GenerationalWealthBooks.com

I promise once you see how this works using the generational wealth system that your mindset will shift.

You can call it magic or divine or anything else you want to call it. But it's nothing short of miraculous when your mindset takes this important shift.

I can't wait for you to see this mindset shift in action.

You don't have to believe me right now. All you have to do is follow the 5 steps of the system and let the system prove to you that it works. The magic and miracles will come.

How I Developed the Generational Wealth System

I've spent a great deal of my life searching for how to be successful. I also have spent my life in church and studying God's word. And while this book isn't about teaching you about God's word, I've been greatly influenced by His word and my faith.

My journey to creating generational wealth started when I read the Bible verse I mentioned in the first chapter. I'd already spent years studying and working on being more successful and making money. But when I read this verse, everything clicked into place in my mind. And since that time, I've worked on the generational wealth system in this book.

Here's the Bible verse again:

Proverbs 13:22

"A good man leaveth an inheritance to his children's children."

(Full disclosure: This is just the first part of the verse. The rest of the verse doesn't change the meaning of the first part of the verse.)

I have children, but I don't have any grandchildren yet. And when I read this verse and took a realistic look at my life, I didn't have much to leave my children, much less anything to leave for my grandchildren. So I decided it was time to do something about it.

Free 7-day generational wealth course at
GenerationalWealthBooks.com

I put together things I learned from a wide range of people and sources to develop a system that had the best possible odds of working that I could develop. I tested and refined and adjusted the system. The end result is in this book.

While this final generational wealth system was put together by me, I used things I learned from others over the years. In this chapter I recognize the biggest contributors to my success and my system.

Dan Kennedy has been the biggest influence on my success. Dan isn't quite retired at this point, but he's close. He wrote about a system he and Foster Hibbard taught decades ago dividing your income into piles, including a percentage to give away (or make the world a better place.)

I've learned a lot more about success from Dan Kennedy over the years. I've been reading his books and studying his material for at least 25 years. But part of the idea for my system came directly from what he and Foster Hibbard taught.

The next big influence on my system was Jim Rohn. Jim taught a system he called 70/30. It's basically the same as the 70-10-10-10 part of my generational wealth system. I've expanded each part of it in their chapters in this book and added the plus one part.

Jim Rohn passed away in 2009, but you can still read his books. Here's an overview of his 70/30 system so you can compare it to my system:

Jim Rohn was a renowned motivational speaker and author who was known for his insights on personal development and success. He believed that financial success was not just about making money, but also about managing it wisely. His 70/30 system is one of his most popular financial strategies, and it has helped many people achieve financial freedom over the years.

The 70/30 rule is a financial system. The rule aims to help you achieve financial independence by dividing your income into two parts: 70% for necessities and luxuries, and 30% for savings, investments, and charity.

To apply the 70/30 rule, you need discipline and a plan. Here are the steps you can follow:

1. Calculate your after-tax income.
2. Allocate 70% of your income for necessities and luxuries, such as rent, food, transportation, and entertainment.
3. Allocate 10% of your income for savings. This will help you build an emergency fund and achieve your financial goals.
4. Allocate 10% of your income for investments. This will help you grow your wealth and secure your future.
5. Allocate 10% of your income for charity. This will help you give back to your community and make a positive impact on the world.

Free 7-day generational wealth course at
GenerationalWealthBooks.com

As you learn about my system in the following chapters, you'll see similarities to Rohn's system. But you'll also see that I tweaked them in ways that make them work better for me.

Many things influenced the plus one part in my generational wealth system. The key to most important things in life is taking action. You need to know what to do, which I'm teaching you in this book. But if you don't take consistent action, even if you know what you need to do you won't get far.

Every part of my generational wealth system is equally important. The four parts about what to do with your money are important. But if you skip the fifth part, the plus 1 part, you're going to find it almost impossible to succeed.

A Deep Dive into 70%

The first step of the system is using 70% or less of your income to pay for all of your expenses, needs, and wants. But don't panic if you don't see any way you can make this work. You can start right where you are right now, and build toward the perfect system.

I'll cover what to do if you're struggling to make this work shortly. For now, please focus on the details in this chapter.

70% isn't a magic number. It's just a number that is realistic for many people to start with if they stretch. And it leaves a nice round 30% to split 3 ways for everything else.

But eventually 50% and 20% and 10% will be realistic. In other words, when you create enough wealth to live on 10% of your income, your wealth grows faster and you can use more of your wealth making the world a better place.

But, what if you can't possibly start with 70%?

The generational wealth system is designed to start where you are now. If you can't live on 70% of your income, determine what percentage of your income you can survive on right now.

Go through every penny you spend every month and cut out anything you don't have to have.

Is creating generational wealth important enough to you to cut out a few things?

I've worked with many people who claim they can't live on 100% of their income. And if you truly believe this, you have to start using this system right now. It's your best opportunity to get out of the rut you're in.

Here's exactly what I do with anyone starting this system I work with who struggles to make ends meet.

They start with 97-1-1-1. 1% usually isn't a lot, but it's more than nothing.

If you make $1,500 a month, you live on $1,455 a month, and have three piles of $15 each for the other 3 parts.

I know $15 isn't much. But you have to follow the system, so you set aside $15 in each of the other 3 areas of the system.

You're going to learn more about the other three piles in the following chapters. But for now, you use $15 to make more money, you save $15, and you give away the last $15.

If you have to start at 97-1-1-1 you focus on making money with the $15 you set aside for making more money and on making money in your plus 1 hour each day.

Your goal is to combine your money for making money and your daily time to grow your income. As your income grows, you can live on less than 97%.

Maybe the next step is doing 91-3-3-3, and you keep increasing your income. And then you get to 85-5-5-5 and then 79-7-7-7.

You keep working the system and increasing your income until you get to 70-10-10-10.

Once you get the system working efficiently you continue moving the percentage you live on down and increase the percentages you invest and use to make more money.

Your ultimate system might be a little different than mine. But here's my ultimate system numbers:

10-40-40-10

My goal is to live on 10% of my income, use 40% to make more money, invest 40%, and give away 10%.

It's entirely up to you how much you give away and use to make the world better. But realize that as you make more money, the value of the 10% goes up.

If you make $10,000 a month and use 10% to make the world better, you're using $1,000 a month. But if you make $100,000 a month, the same 10% is now $10,000.

If you can, start with 70-10-10-10. But if you can't, start wherever you are now and change your percentages as you increase your income.

Free 7-day generational wealth course at
GenerationalWealthBooks.com

This chapter is the simplest part of the generational wealth system. It's not exactly easy, but it's simple.

Do whatever it takes to get started, and adjust as you can.

Now, let's get into the 10% you use to make more money.

Use Money to Make Money

Using money to make money can be challenging. If you're not entrepreneurial minded, it can be overwhelming. But don't worry if you can't imagine how you can use money to make money.

I'm going to give you several ideas in this chapter. Use the ideas to see if anything resonates with you. You don't have to use any of the ideas in this chapter. But hopefully at least one of the ideas gets you thinking about something you can do.

Here's another important point about using money to make money. There are 1,000's of ways to use money to make money. You only have to find 1 to get started.

And as you start making money in 1 way, you figure out other ways to use money to make money. Eventually you might develop dozens of ways to use money to make money.

But don't get overwhelmed at the beginning. Find 1 way to use money to make money and build on that.

Here are some ideas for using money to make money:

Buy – Improve – Profit

Many people try to buy things for a low price and sell them for a higher price. And there's nothing wrong with this. But there's often a lot of competition.

But not as many people buy something and improve it in some way, and then sell it for a profit. This can take many different forms. And sometimes you can buy 2 or more things, combine them in some way, and then sell for a profit.

I used to buy gemstones, attach findings to them, add a leather necklace, and sell them for profit.

I also used to buy bulk inventory of used books and sell them online 1 by 1.

The first example with the gemstones, I bought the stones, findings, and necklaces, combined them, and sold them.

In the second example, I bought in quantity for a low price, and profited from selling individual books. This was several years ago, but I bought books in bulk for roughly 50 cents each delivered. Some of the books didn't sell, but I sold most books for $2 to $10 each. And every once in a while I'd sell one for considerably more.

You can still make money buying books in bulk and reselling them, but it's more challenging to find bulk used books that haven't been picked over. You don't want to buy books that won't sell.

Specialize in a Market

I still do this on a small scale, but at 1 time I did this a lot. I know a lot about a few specific markets that interest me, including what things sell for.

I check these markets frequently, and when I see things that are underpriced I buy them. Then I sell them for a higher price.

For example, I collect books by Roger Zelazny. I used to check eBay, ABE, and other places daily for his books. I knew exactly which books were valuable and how much I could sell them for.

Often I bought the books and then sold them on the same market for a higher price. Or I would buy on ABE and sell on eBay.

This type of hustle is competitive. And you have to be a true specialist on the pricing and market. Plus, in a small market like Roger Zelazny books, you might only find a good deal once every week or two.

But I specialize in other markets as well. If you specialize in 20 or 40 markets that interest you, you can use this method to make money.

The problem with the ideas I've introduced so far is they're hard or impossible to scale beyond a certain point. But when you're getting started, these are things just about anyone can do.

Used books aren't the only way to do something like this. I like books so it fits a way I liked to hustle. Think of things you're interested in, and then see if there's a way to make money.

And there are 1,000's of markets like my example of Zelazny books. Again, what are you interested in. Use these examples to get your mind working towards ways to use money to make money.

Scalable Possibilities

You need to start using money to make money the fastest way you can. This means that for many people, doing something like I just covered is the short-term answer.

But you also want to start thinking about longer term answers and scalability.

Here's a quick overview of several longer term possibilities. And most of them are more scalable.

Start an information marketing business.

An information marketing business is 1 of my favorite recommendations for using money to make more money.

Starting an information marketing business can be done with little investment, and the potential returns are huge.

Information marketing businesses are also scalable. The main reason why information marketing businesses are scalable is because you do the work once, or pay someone else to do the work, and then you can sell the information forever.

A wide range of things can be included in an information marketing business. Some things include books, reports, courses, videos, and audios.

Free 7-day generational wealth course at
GenerationalWealthBooks.com

Most people make the mistake of thinking nobody will pay for anything they know. But people pay for information every day.

And most people have some specialized knowledge that someone else is willing to pay for.

For example, I've been automatically figuring things like gross profit, net profit, margins, etc in businesses most of my adult life. But many people, even many who own businesses, don't know how to do this. I often forget that I automatically do some things that others want to know how to do.

I help many of my clients develop and expand information marketing businesses as a part of helping them create generational wealth.

Start a blog or web site.

It's easier than ever to start your own web site or blog. You can buy a domain and hosting and set up blog software, like Wordpress, in 15 minutes or less.

When I started online, it took over 24 hours sometimes to get a page published. Now when I publish a post, it's live online in seconds.

Web sites and blogs are somewhat like an information marketing business, in that you publish content and it can make you money forever.

But it usually takes longer for a blog or web site to start producing revenue. On the other hand, if you stick with it long enough and continue creating valuable content, you can make a lot of money with web sites and blogs.

Start a YouTube channel.

Few things pay better long-term financially than getting your face and message in front of people. And YouTube is a free way to build your audience.

Many people are afraid to show their face on camera. They think people might not like them, or they're nervous.

Instead of worrying about how many people might not like you, focus on the people that are going to like you.

Plenty of people don't find my information interesting. Some don't like the way I talk. And I'm sure some people make fun of me.

But I don't worry about all of those people. Because there are plenty of people who learn a lot from me. And I resonate with many people. And I help a lot of people with the information I provide.

Like a web site or blog, a YouTube channel requires ongoing work and content creation to grow.

But you're building an audience. And the audience you grow gets to know you and will support you over time.

Don't be afraid to get in front of the camera and get started. I mess up in videos all of the time. And most of the time when I mess up, I'm the only person it bothers.

If you're watching 1 of my videos and you're learning valuable lessons about how to create generational wealth and change your life, do you care if I make a small mistake now and then?

As long as you're providing valuable information and helping people, your audience is going to understand that you're human and might make an occasional mistake.

Become an author.

Becoming an author isn't for everyone. But if you love to write and you're good at it, you can write a book and sell it forever.

How many books do you own that were written by authors 10 or 20 or even more years ago?

I've had books published by traditional publishers and I've self published books. And I've made money on both types of books.

If you can figure out how to sell your books, self publishing might be the way to go. But if you write in some categories, like popular fiction or romance, and you're good, you might be able to land a big book deal with a traditional publisher.

Warning

Notice that I haven't mentioned anything about buying a franchise business or a business opportunity or buying an established business in this section.

I don't have anything against any of these things. And eventually 1 of these types of businesses may be a big part of your generational wealth creation.

But I don't recommend them when you're starting your journey unless you have a lot of experience already.

Too often you're creating a job instead of building much wealth. If you want to create a job, that's fine. But it needs to be a conscious decision.

Here's an example:

Years ago I ran a hardware store. I liked it, but it was a lot of work.

I considered buying a hardware store because I knew how to make a hardware store profitable. I still know how to make money with a hardware store.

But I decided it wasn't the right path for me at the time. All I would have done is created a job for myself.

I might buy a hardware store, or multiple hardware stores, in the future. But not to work in them. Now I'd buy them, put the things in place I know that work and makes money, and let someone else run them.

Notice the difference between working in your business and on your business. This is an important mindset shift you need to think about if you want to create generational wealth.

Save and Invest in the Future

You're living on 70% of your income and you're using 10% of your income to make more money. The next step of the generational wealth system is to save and invest 10% of your income.

When you start, the easiest thing to do is put 10% of your income in a saving account.

Savings accounts don't pay much interest, so you're not going to leave the money you save in a saving account forever.

But you need to keep the money somewhere until you have enough to invest in larger opportunities.

If you have to start with 97-1-1-1 until you increase your income, you can put your savings and investment money in an envelope in a drawer until it builds up.

When you're starting your generational wealth journey, it's not important where you put your money. What's important is saving.

The practice of saving and investing helps you create an important mindset shift. Even if the money you save and invest doesn't grow much at first, the fact that it is growing is great.

I track my investments every day because it makes me happy to see the progress. And when you see frequent progress, it helps you stay on track.

This book isn't about telling you how or where to invest your money. I'm not a financial advisor. But I'm going to give you some thoughts about it that have helped me over the years.

I don't invest in anything I don't understand. And I never let anyone else make my investment decisions for me.

People lost a lot of money to pyramid schemes like the Bernie Madoff scandal. But the people who investigated and understood how Madoff was supposedly making money quickly saw that it couldn't last.

The most well-known and successful investor of our time, Warren Buffet, has a two rule system that's often quoted.

He says rule number 1 is never lose money. He says rule 2 is see rule 1.

I've invested in a lot of different things over the years. I've lost money at times, but I've learned from every loss.

The biggest mistake I've made is investing in things I don't understand. I've learned to never do that again.

You can make money in a wide range of investments. But in almost every type of investment you can also lose money.

You need to identify at least 1 way you think you'd like to invest and get as much education as possible.

For example many people make money in real estate investing. But some people lose money in real estate investing.

Some people make money in the stock market, but many people lose money.

Some people make money investing in businesses, and some people lose money.

The list goes on and on.

Don't invest in anything you don't understand. But if you don't understand how an investment works, you can study and learn.

I'm currently investing in the stock market using options. I always heard that options are risky, so I ignored them for years.

But I eventually decided to learn more about them, so I went into an active learning mode. I read over 30 books about the stock market, investing, and options.

Now I completely understand how options work and know how to trade them profitably.

But I made many mistakes along the way.

Years ago I bought some penny stocks without having any idea what I was doing. I lost every penny I invested.

The important thing to learn from my experience is I didn't study and learn enough before investing.

You probably know how a savings account works. You give the bank money, and they use your money to make money. The bank gives you back a small percentage of the money they make using your money.

The next level of investment with a bank is a CD, or certificate of deposit. A CD works much the same way as a savings account, but you agree to give the bank your money for a minimum amount of time.

At first, savings accounts and CDs are ok. Your money is relatively safe and you make a little interest.

But once you build up some savings, it's time to find better investment vehicles.

I can't tell you how much you need to accumulate before investing outside of a bank. But as a loose rule of thumb, shoot for at least $10,000 before venturing out.

Spend the time while you're building your investment capital to learn more about what you want to invest in.

I'm going to let you in on a secret.

There's no shame in leaving your investment money in safe and low interest vehicles if that's what you decide to do.

If you're not comfortable investing your money elsewhere, then don't invest it elsewhere.

As long as you're not losing money and you're gaining some interest, you're on the right track.

And if you're following the rest of the generational wealth system, you're still going to make big gains.

If you learn how to use money to make money, like I covered in the last chapter, and you're not comfortable investing money elsewhere, you might eventually decide to use your savings and investing accounts to make money the same way.

Here are some general rules to use with your savings and investing accounts:

1. Don't lose money.
2. Limit your risk.
3. Look for opportunities where your upside far outweighs your risk.
4. Consistently build your savings and investments.
5. Keep a small percentage of your savings and investments liquid. This means keeping a percentage of your money in a way you can quickly access it in case of an emergency.

I made too many risky investments earlier in my life. Now I carefully calculate the risk of any investment before I make it.

When I take risks with my investment capital, I look for limited risk and big possible upside or profit.

Make the World a Better Place

I'm sure it seems to many people that giving money away is the opposite of creating generational wealth. And until you start using your money to make the world a better place, it's hard to understand how this works.

But it does work. When you use a portion of your income to make the world a better place in some way, you almost always end up with more than you started with in 1 way or another.

This has happened to me so many times that I'm afraid not to use a portion of my income improving the world because I might miss out on something important.

I'm a pastor at an old country church, so I'm quite familiar with tithing. But what I'm talking about in this section doesn't have to be tithing. In fact, I tell my congregation that they should support their church, but they can and should use part of their money doing something important to them.

In other words, they should strive to make the world a better place.

Here's an example:

We have things called blessing boxes where I live. People put food in these blessing boxes and anyone who has a need can take the food from the boxes. My youngest daughter feels this is important. So, often when we go grocery shopping she asks if we can buy 10 or 20 cans of food to put in the blessing box.

Let me tell you something important. If you want to make the world a better place, give someone who's hungry something to eat.

It touches me at a deep level when my daughter does this. I'm fighting back tears writing about it. She knows how blessed we are because we always have plenty of food. And she knows she can help someone by putting food in a blessing box.

Now, back to the 10% in the generational wealth system you use to make the world a better place.

Some of you reading this have already decided you're not giving anything away. You're welcome to use this system any way you want. But I'm warning you that you're going to have a much easier path to creating generational wealth if you follow the plan. And the plan says use 10% for good.

I don't use some of my money making the world a better place in hopes of a big return. I do it because helping a single person makes the world better. And helping a single person can change their life.

But I've seen giving work out to the givers benefit so many times that I know it's not a coincidence.

You can believe this is because of God or because it helps shift your mental state in generating wealth or because of something else. I know what I believe, but this isn't about forcing my beliefs on you.

You can call this phenomenon anything you want. But I urge you to do it so you can become a believer too.

Now, the benefits aren't always the same thing you give. And sometimes the benefits don't show up for a long time. But they always come back to you.

And here's another important point. Nobody gets to tell you how to use your money to make the world a better place. Not me or anyone else. You decide what you want to do and do it. Whatever is important to you or strikes your heart as important is important.

Set aside 10% of your income and use it to make the world a better place. As your generational wealth grows, you can do more and more to improve the world.

This is one of the main reasons I'm sharing the generational wealth system. If enough people learn how to create generational wealth and use 10% of their income to make the world better, the world will benefit a lot.

I want the world to be better for my kids and future generations. The generational wealth system is the best way for this to happen.

So, get out there and make the world a better place.

Plus 1

The plus 1 part of the generational wealth system is where the magic happens. While every part of this system is important, the plus 1 part makes everything else in the system better.

Plus 1 means creating generational wealth at least 1 hour every day.

What you do with your plus 1 hour depends on what your current goals are and where you are in your journey to generational wealth.

When you're starting your journey, your plus 1 hour might be spent using money to make money. Or, if you're starting at 97-1-1-1 instead of at 70-10-10-10, you might work an extra hour at your current job to make more money.

If you've started creating generational wealth and have created multiple streams of income, you might use your plus 1 hour to manage your businesses.

The plus 1 hour is the minimum commitment every day. At first, you might not be able to commit more than an hour every day. But as you work the system and increase your income, you can commit more time to creating generational wealth.

Unless you 100% love what you're doing now, eventually with this system you can work more on the things that are important to you and that make you more money.

Free 7-day generational wealth course at
GenerationalWealthBooks.com

I know you're probably busy. And on one hand an hour a day might sound reasonable. But on the other hand some days get so busy that it's difficult to find an hour.

But your journey to generational wealth is important. So you don't find an hour a day to work on it. You make an hour every day to work on it.

I schedule my plus 1 hour first every day.

At first, I had to get up an hour early to make sure I got my hour in every day on creating generational wealth. I still try to do it the first thing every day to make sure the day doesn't get hectic and make it difficult. But I made a commitment to never go to bed without doing at least an hour on creating generational wealth every day.

Here's the real secret to success with the generational wealth system. Make a decision that you're going to use the generational wealth system, no matter what. Then make a commitment to follow through on your decision, no matter what. Finally, never give up, no matter what.

1. Decide.
2. Commit.
3. Never give up.

I know it sounds simple. But this system works. So, you have a good system. Now all you need to do is decide, commit, and never give up.

I recommend taking a moment right now and decide you're going to use this system no matter what. Then commit to using the system, no matter what.

The reason why I include these 3 important steps here is because you're going to be tempted to skip your plus 1 hour eventually.

You can't skip your plus 1 hour.

If you know you can't do an hour, you have to do the hour before. You can't make an hour up later. If you give in and skip an hour once, you're likely to do it again.

If you truly want to create generational wealth, you're going to do everything in your power to get your plus 1 hour in every day. Once you're well on your way to creating generational wealth you can plan a day off ahead of time.

What I do most weeks is plan Sunday off, so I make sure I get an extra hour in the week before. Of course, I usually work more than an hour a day on my generational wealth now, but in the beginning I didn't have extra time.

If your days are so full that you don't see where you can get an hour, you have 2 choices. You can give up now, or you can make an hour every day.

If you have to, get up an hour early every day. If you have a lot of interruptions, working an hour before everyone else is awake is a great idea.

Track every minute of your day for a few weeks to see exactly where you're spending your time. Even if you have to do 15 minutes in the morning, 30 minutes at lunch, and 15 minutes before bed, make an hour for your wealth creation system every day.

While I don't watch a lot of television, I still watch it some. And I schedule time for my family every day. I still do the things that are important to me. But I've cut out almost everything that's not important to me and that is a waste of time.

I'm not telling you what should be important to you. You decide what's important and what's not important. Then schedule the important things first, starting with your plus 1 hour every day.

If you want to change your financial situation, you have to start doing something different. Changing your financial future, and the financial future of your family and future generations, starts with the 5 steps in this system.

With only 1 hour every day and the other 4 steps of the generational wealth system, you can change your life. 1 hour a day is a small price to pay to start creating generational wealth.

I still waste at least an hour every day doing things that aren't productive. And I track my time closely. You can make an hour every day, as long as making an hour is important enough.

Free 7-day generational wealth course at
GenerationalWealthBooks.com

Is creating generational wealth more important than watching television? Only you can decide what you want. To me, creating generational wealth is more important than watching an extra hour of television.

Is creating generational wealth more important than spending an hour on social media? Again, the choice is yours.

Remember the 3 important steps:

1. Decide.
2. Commit.
3. Never give up.

Work Your Generational Wealth System Every Day

Is creating generational wealth important to you?

If you're still reading, I think it's safe to say that creating generational wealth is important to you.

And if creating generational wealth is important to you, it's important enough to work on every day.

The system includes at least an hour every day in the plus 1 part. So, to make sure you work your generational wealth system every day, all you have to do is follow the system.

But you will face challenges. And the odds are high that you're going to want to give up at least once.

And I can guarantee that you're going to face days where you just don't feel like working on your generational wealth.

When you have days where you don't want to work on your generational wealth, there's only 1 way to handle them.

You have to work on your generational wealth anyway.

I've had days where everything seems to fall apart. And you will too. But you have to do something towards creating generational wealth every day.

Here's an example:

Free 7-day generational wealth course at
GenerationalWealthBooks.com

1 of my children was sick and I had to take her to the emergency room. I didn't have the chance to work on my generational wealth in the morning like I usually do, because I had to take care of her.

As a side note, notice that creating generational wealth is 1 of my top priorities in life. But it's not a priority over my family.

I know my priorities and I know what order my priorities are in. I made a conscious choice of my priorities list and order so I never have to think about what's more important.

I'm not telling you what your priority list and order is supposed to be. You get to decide your priorities and their order.

What I am telling you is you need to make a priority list and put it in order so you don't have to think about what's more important.

If you're interested in my priority list, I'll share it with you.

1. God
2. My family
3. Generational wealth
4. My health
5. Freedom

When my daughter was sick and needed me to take care of her, it came before creating generational wealth.

Free 7-day generational wealth course at
GenerationalWealthBooks.com

Back to the example:

I took her to the emergency room and we ended up being gone all day. By the time I got home, all we wanted to do was collapse and rest.

But I still worked on my generational wealth that day. I didn't get to work on it for an hour, so I worked an extra hour the next day.

Here's what I did to work on my generational wealth while sitting in the emergency room.

Once my daughter was taken care of and resting, waiting on lab results, I got out my phone and sent a couple of emails to people I was working with to use money to make money.

I also reviewed my progress and made plans for the next day. I also spent time thinking about what else I needed to do to keep moving towards generational wealth.

It wasn't much, but I did make progress that day on my generational wealth plan.

Make a conscious decision to work your generational wealth plan every day. Commit to working your plan every day, no matter what.

Generational Wealth Challenges and How to Overcome Them

You're going to face many challenges as you're creating generational wealth.

The biggest challenge most people I work with face at first is learning how to make adjustments to live on 70% of their income. I've addressed this challenge already. Start where you are and build up to 70% if you need to.

I know you're going to face challenges because I've faced a lot of challenges on my journey. And my clients face challenges.

But you can work through and overcome the challenges you're going to face.

I can't list every possible challenge you might face. But I can give you a few tools you can use when you face challenges.

1 of the best tools you can use when you face challenges on your journey to creating generational wealth is getting help from someone that has faced the same challenges.

I cover how to get help in another chapter you're going to read soon.

Another tool you can use is a system or framework I use with most of my clients. Here's the system I use.

I help my clients with many things, including creating generational wealth. But another important thing I teach is a goal system.

While this book isn't exactly about a goal system, the system I teach does help with creating generational wealth. So, I'm going to share a quick overview of the goal system here because it will help you on your journey to generational wealth. And this goal system helps you recognize and overcome challenges.

Before giving you the goal system, you might have noticed that I like to use systems. You're reading about the generational wealth system and now I'm introducing you to my goal system.

I use systems as frameworks and guides when I'm doing something important. When I can put everything into a system, it helps me stay on track, recognize challenges, and overcome the challenges.

When I create and use a system, it also does 2 other important things.

1. Creating and using systems gives me confidence. I'm more comfortable when I'm using a proven system.
2. When you use a proven system like the systems I'm sharing with you in this book, it greatly increases your chance of success. A proven system has step by step details and has worked for other people. And if you use the same system

or systems, you have a much higher chance to succeed than when you don't use a system.

I've called this goal system many things, but my favorite is the goal system that never fails.

Here are the steps to the goal system.

1. Determine exactly what you want.
2. Determine exactly why you want it.
3. Find other people who have accomplished the same thing you want to achieve.
4. Study what they have done.
5. Create a detailed, step by step plan, of what others have done to achieve what you want to do.
6. Determine if you're willing to pay the price to achieve what you want.
7. Break the steps down to small parts.
8. Do the first step right now.
9. Continue taking small steps every single day.
10. Review your plan and progress every week.
11. Adjust your plan based on what you've accomplished and what you've learned.
12. Never give up.

I'm sure you can see how my goal system overlaps with my generational wealth creation system.

Please use this goal system with the generational wealth creation system. But you can use this goal system in any area of your life.

Free 7-day generational wealth course at
GenerationalWealthBooks.com

I know I've told you this many times, but the most important thing you need to overcome any challenges you face creating generational wealth is never give up.

You have the systems and information you need. The only ingredient you need to bring to the table is the never give up, no matter what, determination and attitude.

When to Start?

I love this question.

When someone asks me when they should start, the answer is easy and it's always the same.

You should start right now. And when I say right now, I mean right this second.

And you need to keep starting right now every day.

In the next chapter you're going to learn a simple way to get started immediately. You don't have to start the way I suggest in the next chapter.

But if you're hesitant or stuck, it's a simple step by step way to get started on your journey to creating generational wealth.

I'm going to share a bit of great news with you. As you're reading this book, you've already started on your journey to creating generational wealth.

A big part of the generational wealth system includes learning what to do and not do.

Some things you have to learn by doing them. But as you're reading this book and learning about this system, you've already started on your journey.

The next step is just as important as any other step. You have to get started right away every day.

So, get started right now. And get started every day. As you stack day after day of progress, you get closer to your goal.

How to Start Immediately

You know what you need to do to start your journey to creating generational wealth. You have the proven system you need.

But I know that it can be scary and intimidating to start something this big and important.

If you've already started using what you've learned in this book, you can skip this chapter.

But if you need a little boost, here's a step by step way to get started.

1. Determine exactly how much money you have coming in every month.
2. List every penny you spend every month.
3. Determine everything you spend money on that you can live without.
4. Using the information gathered so far, determine what percentage of your income you can live on.
5. Split the remaining money 3 ways and set your beginning percentages.
6. Remember that you don't have to stress about it if you can't start at 70-10-10-10. Start where you are and as your income increases you work toward 70-10-10-10.
7. Research ways you can use money to make money. When you're starting, focus on making a profit, even if it's small. You want to increase your income any way you can, especially if you're not starting at 70-10-10-10.

Free 7-day generational wealth course at GenerationalWealthBooks.com

8. Start your plus 1 today. Use your hour to do the things listed above. And tomorrow, use your hour to start increasing your income.

9. Determine where you're going to put the money for saving and investing. At first it can be an envelope in a drawer or a saving account. Don't worry about long-term investing until you build up your savings for investing.

10. Determine what you want to do to make the world better. Even if you only start with $50 or $100 a month, you can buy canned food for a food bank or support a cause that's important to you.

11. Make a list of small steps you can do to advance your journey towards creating generational wealth. The steps don't have to be big. With small steps, you can make sure you're making progress every day.

12. Don't be afraid of spending time learning what you don't know. You're going to spend the rest of your life learning.

13. On the other hand, don't get so involved in learning and researching that you never start taking action.

14. Start now. Start right this second.

Action and Consistency Are the Keys that Unlock Generational Wealth

I read a quote that said what you do consistently is more important than what you know.

While you need to know what to do, I agree that what you do consistently is important. In fact, action and consistency, or taking consistent action, is the key to unlocking generational wealth.

You have the information you need to know to start creating generational wealth. You hold in your hands a proven system that others have used to create generational wealth.

But knowing how the system works isn't enough to unlock true generational wealth.

You have to take action. And you have to consistently take action.

Consistent action is built into this system. The plus 1 requires daily action and progress.

Let me put all of this a different way.

The 3 things you need to create generational wealth are:

- A proven system.
- Take action on your proven system.
- Consistently work your system.

If you want to unlock generational wealth, take consistent action.

I know this sounds simple. I like simple things. That's why I develop systems.

Creating generational wealth is simple in many ways. This doesn't mean that creating generational wealth is easy.

But you have a simple system that only requires consistent action.

Celebrate the simplicity and start taking action today. And take action every day.

The Power of Accountability

I'm giving you every tip and trick I know in this book to make sure you have the best chance to create generational wealth.

And the information in this chapter is 1 of the most important tools you can use to create generational wealth.

I call it the power of accountability because accountability is 1 of the most powerful things you can use to help you achieve your goals.

I use these same methods in everything important I do.

When you're working on a big important goal like creating generational wealth, you need to find a way to be held accountable.

Accountability is simply doing what you say you're going to do.

This isn't an ethical discussion in any way. But how many times have you told yourself you were going to do something and didn't do it?

It's easy to lie to yourself.

Creating generational wealth is so important that you need to find a way to be held accountable.

The easiest way to use the power of accountability is getting someone to hold you accountable.

There are many different ways to do this. But the easiest way is to find someone you don't want to disappoint that's willing to help you.

Tell them what you're doing and why you're doing it. Ask if they are willing to help you.

Schedule a regular time to discuss your plans and what you've accomplished.

If you can find someone else who wants to create generational wealth, you can hold each other accountable.

You don't have to talk every day or go into deep detail about what you're doing. Once a week is what I recommend at first.

Or you could exchange an email every day.

Eventually you might move to speaking once every 2 weeks, but I don't recommend this until you've made a lot of progress and have the habit of following through on your plan every day.

Most of my clients use me for accountability. I also help them in other ways, including with all of the parts of the generational wealth system.

But we usually open each call with a quick review of what they've accomplished and what they're going to accomplish between now and our next phone call.

I also have people on my team that are accountability coaches. They know my system inside and out, but people use them mainly for accountability. (Working with 1 of my team is a smaller investment than working directly with me.)

It's also possible to use someone on my team for accountability and occasionally schedule a call with me to go help with bumps in the road.

I want to make it clear that you don't need to work with me or someone on my team to use the power of accountability. But we're here if you need help. I cover more about this in the next chapter.

Please don't skip the power of accountability. Even if you're the most disciplined person in the world, find someone to use as an accountability person.

Sometimes you just need to talk to someone for a minute who knows what you're doing and why you're doing it.

If you can find someone who wants to create generational wealth, buy them a copy of this book or have them buy a copy and you can take the journey together. Or at least get them to take the free 7 day generational wealth course.

I cover more about how to get the free 7 day course in a later chapter. It's open to everyone because I want as many people as possible to learn this system and create generational wealth and make the world a better place.

Free 7-day generational wealth course at
GenerationalWealthBooks.com

How to Get Help Creating Generational Wealth

As you've read through this book you learned I work with people helping them with the generational wealth system.

You also learned that I have people on my team that are available as accountability coaches.

But before you make an investment into getting help creating generational wealth, spend some time reading this book and learning the system.

I also recommend taking the 7 day generational wealth course. I cover how to access the course for free in another chapter later in this book.

But if you're ready to take the next step and get help from me or my team, here's more information.

I love working with people and helping them create generational wealth and with their businesses.

If you want to work with me directly, complete details about my current availability are listed at GenerationalWealthBooks.com/Strategy

Working with me starts with a 20 minute strategy call. And a 20 minute strategy call is all some people need.

At the end of the call we can talk about your options if you want continuing help. I usually work with people every week or 2 weeks. And I work with people 20 minutes a call, 30 minutes a call, or 60 minutes a call.

If you're interested in working with an accountability coach on my team, you can get more information about how it works at GenerationalWealthBooks.com/Coach

Teaching Your Kids How to Create and Maintain Generational Wealth

Imagine if someone you trusted had introduced you to the generational wealth system included in this book when you were 16 or 18 years old.

And imagine if you trusted them enough to start using the system at that time.

How different would your life be right now?

Kids have a tremendous advantage over most of us. They have more time than most of us.

But most kids also have a hard time figuring out what's important and what to do. As we grow older and gain experience, we often see things differently.

I want my kids to have the best, as I'm sure you want for your kids. And of course, this doesn't have to be only about kids. It's about anyone you love.

You also want your kids to be able to maintain and grow the generational wealth you create for them.

I don't think I'm the only parent that has this problem. But sometimes my kids don't think I know much.

So, if I give them good advice they often ignore it. But if someone else, who they trust, gives them the same good advice, they think it's excellent advice.

Free 7-day generational wealth course at
GenerationalWealthBooks.com

Knowing this is a possibility, I've used other people to introduce a few pieces of good advice over the years to my kids. They're a little older now, so they're more likely to listen to my good advice than when they were younger.

The best way to teach your kids how to create and maintain generational wealth is to get them involved.

The system for creating generational wealth is the same no matter your age. So, if you can get them to read a book, they can read this book.

Or you can buy them a copy of the generational wealth book for kids. Details are available on the site at GenerationalWealthBooks.com

Another way to get your kids involved is use them as accountability partners. And never discount ideas or advice from a kid.

While kids can be wrong about a lot of stuff, as adults we can also be wrong about a lot of stuff.

Kids look at the world and things in a different way than adults do. And sometimes a kid can give you a solution that you would never come up with yourself.

Once your kids learn how to create generational wealth, they won't have trouble maintaining it. In fact, as they mature they're going to grow the generational wealth.

And as they grow the generational wealth, they're going to continue making the world a better place for everyone.

What Generational Wealth Is Not

The reason why you want to create generational wealth is personal. But you should know why you want to create generational wealth.

In other words, what is your why?

Knowing exactly why you want to create generational wealth is important. Knowing your why, or why's, help you achieve what you want.

It's easy to skip this chapter and say you want to create generational wealth to be rich. But generational wealth is about much more than being rich. In fact, money doesn't have to be the main factor in your generational wealth.

I'm not discounting the money aspect. You need money to do the things you want to do. And it's easier to make the world better when you have more money.

Generational wealth is not about fancy cars and huge houses. If you want those things, you can have them once you create generational wealth. But most people that truly create generational wealth don't waste money on cars they don't need and houses they don't need.

I have two cars, but neither of them is new or very fancy. I live in a nice house, but it's the same house I lived in before I started on my generational wealth journey.

Consider Warren Buffet. He's one of the richest people in the world. He lives in the same house he's lived in for decades. It's a nice house, but he could easily afford a

Free 7-day generational wealth course at
GenerationalWealthBooks.com

mega mansion or several mega mansions if he wanted them.

This all ties back into your why or whys.

Let me share my whys with you to give you an example.

I'm creating generational wealth for the following reasons:

- I want to make the world a better place for my kids and descendants.
- I don't want stress that comes from not having enough money.
- Generational wealth means freedom to me.
- Most of all, I do everything I do for my family and me.

Notice that none of my reasons fit in the getting rich category. But all of my reasons why are directly related to creating generational wealth. I don't have to have billions to fulfill my whys.

Spend as much time as you need determining your reasons why you want to create generational wealth. The good news is there are no right or wrong answers.

But if the only reason you can think of is having more money, the odds are stacked against you.

If you're struggling, make a list of everything you plan to do with your generational wealth. List as many things as you can think of. I recommend starting with at least 100 things.

Some of the things you come up with are going to hit you hard. Listen to what you're feeling as you make your list.

Your main reasons why will jump out at you if you work through this.

Another great thing about your reasons why is they can change over time. And there's nothing wrong with changing your reasons why. Some things that used to be important might not be as important now. And new things might be more important.

How to Get the 7 Day Generational Wealth Course for Free

I created a 7 day generational wealth course as a companion to this book. And there really is a 7 day course. This isn't 1 of those books that promises a course or download and then doesn't provide it.

The course includes some of the same things as you've learned in this book. And it also gives some different examples than in this book.

To access the 7 day generational wealth course for free, visit GenerationalWealthBooks.com

I want to take a minute to clarify something in case you have any questions. I want to sell as many books as possible because I want to help as many people create generational wealth as possible. And the more people out there creating generational wealth, the better we collectively make the world.

If you have received value from this book, please buy some more copies and give them to everyone you care about.

But you can also send them to the sign up page for the 7 day generational wealth course. They don't have to own a copy of this book to sign up for the course. The course isn't the same as this book, but it has a lot of value.

Please let everyone you care about know about the free course so they can learn how to create generational wealth. This way they can learn what the book is about for free, and then decide if the book offers enough value for the small investment it takes to buy the book.

As you know because you bought a copy of this book, I priced it at a low investment. I want everyone to have the opportunity to create generational wealth, so pricing the book at an affordable level allows anyone to afford a copy.

Will You Please Help Me Make the World a Better Place?

I'm looking for as much help as possible making the world a better place. You could say that I'm on a mission.

Will you please help me make the world a better place? I truly appreciate everyone who helps.

Here are some ways you can help:

1. Create generational wealth. Use the system in this book, create generational wealth, and make the world better.
2. Tell everyone you know about the generational wealth system.
3. Send people to the free 7 day course so they can see how and why the system works.
4. Give people you care about copies of this book.
5. Consider leaving a 5 star review of the book on Amazon. People looking for books are more likely to buy books with high reviews and a lot of reviews.

Thank you for your help!

About the Author, Wes Young

Instead of writing the about the author chapter in the same voice most books do, I'm writing in the same voice I use in the rest of the book. I don't include this chapter to make myself sound better than I really am. I include the information in this chapter to show you why you need to take the rest of the book seriously.

The generational wealth system included in this book is so powerful that it changes lives every day. In addition to changing your life, it will change the lives of your kids and everyone else you love in the world.

I know you can use this generational wealth system to improve your life and the lives of everyone you care about because I've done it and I've helped others do it.

I didn't get a head start growing up. My parents always provided love, food, and a home, but they didn't have a lot of money. I have two college degrees but neither of them is from a prestigious university. And very little of what I learned in college has had anything to do with generational wealth.

You don't need a college education to create generational wealth. Ad you don't need to come from old money or family success to create generational wealth.

You already have everything you need to create generational wealth. Use the information in this book to start your journey toward creating generational wealth immediately. And if you need help along the way, see the chapter covering how to get help.

Growing up, I was taught I could accomplish anything I wanted to accomplish. And I'm here to tell you that you can create generational wealth.

The only reason I earned my first college degree, a Bachelor's in Mathematics, was because I went to college to play baseball. My dream growing up was to be a professional baseball player. I was a good baseball player, and I played four years in college. By the time I finished playing I had to face the hard fact that I wasn't going to be a Major League Baseball player.

I turned my attention to learning how to be successful. I've spent years studying success. And I learned that if someone else can be successful, I can be successful too. I simply had to determine what success means to me and model what others do to achieve the same success.

That's what this book covers. I share with you a system to achieve success by creating generational wealth. This system isn't the only system that works. But it's a system that I know works because I've used it and many of my clients use it.

My other degree is a Master's in Business Administration. Having an MBA isn't good or bad. But I found that I learned more about business and success by running businesses than I learned in my studies for my MBA. My MBA has opened some doors for me over the years that might have been more difficult to open, but at this point in my life it's simply a few letters.

My current life includes working on my generational wealth every day, being a pastor at an old country church, teaching my kids about creating generational wealth, enjoying time with my family, writing, and helping others learn how to create generational wealth. I'm available on a limited basis for consulting, as described in the how to get help chapter, and also for speaking engagements on a limited basis. You can contact me through the site for this book.

This book isn't about me. It's about you and what you can do with the rest of your life. I urge you to use everything in this book and start your journey to generational wealth today. There's no better time to start creating generational wealth than right now.

I truly hope you create generational wealth and teach everyone you care about how to do it too. You have the system, now it's up to you. Are you going to use what you know and create generational wealth starting today, or are you going to look back in the future and regret not taking immediate action?

The choice is yours. Make the choice right now and take action.

God Bless You,

Wes Young

Notes:

Notes

Notes

Notes

Wes Young is the pastor at an old country church, an entrepreneur, and a consultant. He works with people from all walks of life helping them create generational wealth using the system and framework included in this book.

If you had a proven system that provided step by step instructions on how to create generational wealth, would you use it? What if the system has been used successfully by others starting right where you are?

What is your definition of generational wealth? Whatever your definition of generational wealth is, *The Simple Step By Step System Anyone Can Use to Create Generational Wealth* book gives you the system and framework to start your journey today.

Here are some highlights of what's covered in this book:

- The Step By Step Generational Wealth System - Page 27
- How to Make Creating Generational Wealth Inevitable - Page 23
- How I Developed the Generational Wealth System - Page 35
- Make the World a Better Place - Page 59
- How to Overcome Generational Wealth Challenges - Page 73
- Teach Your Kids How to Create Generational Wealth - Page 89
- What Generational Wealth Is Not - Page 93
- How to Get a 7 Day Generational Wealth Course for Free - Page 99
- Why I Want You to Create Generational Wealth - Page 13
- The Big Promise - Page 19
- Use Money to Make Money - Page 43
- Invest in the Future - Page 53

Free 7-day generational wealth course at
GenerationalWealthBooks.com